Thank you. Check also our other boo

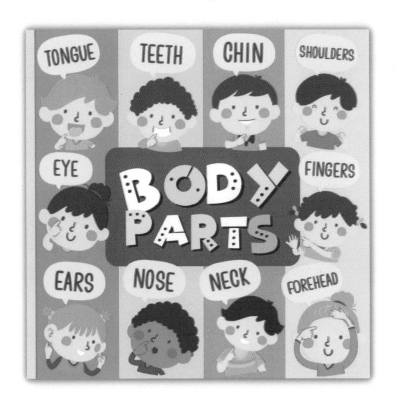

ASIN: B09RLY9CTK

ASIN: B09QP1Y161

Enter this ASIN in the search engine

Ballerina

Misio Publishing

The Ballerina Costume is
the Most Important Part
of the Dance

Ballet Silhouettes

Only Very Good Female Ballet
Dancer is Called Ballerina

Ballet Teaches
the Art of Patience

Among the Basic Steps of Ballet are
Various Jumps, Turns, and Sliding Steps

Ballet Dancers are Incredibly Fit

In Ballet, There are Five Basic Positions of the Feet Numbered One Through Five

Ballet Teaches Self Discipline
and Self Confidence

Pirouettes are One of the Most Commonly-Known Ballet Moves

The First-Ever Prima Ballerina Came from France

The Paris Opera Ballet School
is the Most Famous Ballet
School in the World

The First Ballet Dancers
Were all Men

An Average Ballet Dancer
Wears 50 to 150 Tutus
in Her Lifetime

Dancers Perform Many Movements
which are Unnatural for the Body

A Ballet Dancer Can Show
the Human Body in an Elegant
and Harmonious Way

A Whipped Throw is One of the Most Difficult Turns in Ballet Dance

Swan Lake is Perhaps
the Most Well-Known Ballet

One Ballet Performance
Can Take Up to 5,000
Hours of Practice

Friendship Between Ballerinas
Can Last for Years

The Paris Opera Ballet School
is the Most Famous Ballet
School in the World

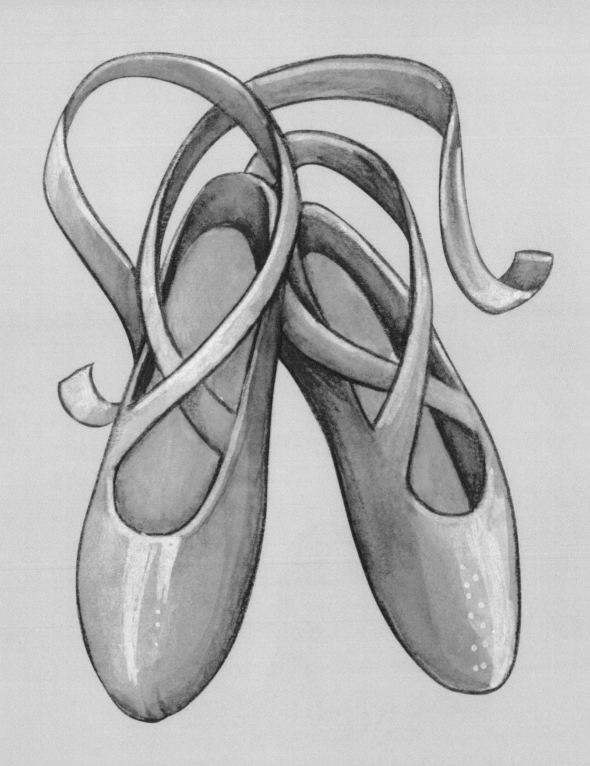

Professional Ballet Dancers
Wear Pointe Shoe

The Word Ballet Comes from
the Word Dance in Latin

The History of Ballet Begins
Around 1500 in Italy

According to Average Statistics,
80% of Ballet Dancers are Women
and 20% are Men

A Single Performance is the
Equivalent of Running
up to 18 Miles

One Ballet Dance Lasts
on Average of Four Hours

Most Ballet Terms are From
the French Language

Printed in Great Britain
by Amazon

23585908R00025